Barbara Bush
LITERACY CHAMPION

BY PATRICIA HUTCHISON

8-28-18   20-

J
B
BUSH, B/HUT

Published by The Child's World®
1980 Lookout Drive • Mankato, MN 56003-1705
800-599-READ • www.childsworld.com

Photographs ©: Charles Tasnadi/AP Images, cover, 1; Robert F. Bukaty/AP Images, 5; Scott Applewhite/AP Images, 6; Everett Collection/Newscom, 9; Courtesy Everett Collection/Rex Features/AP Images, 10; Bob Daugherty/AP Images, 12; Steve Sisney/The Daily Oklahoman/AP Images, 15; Marcy Nighswander/AP Images, 17; AP Images, 18; Gerald Herbert/AP Images, 20

ISBN 9781503823938
LCCN 2017944733

Printed in the United States of America
PA02362

ABOUT THE AUTHOR

Patricia Hutchison has written more than a dozen children's books about history and science. She was a teacher for many years. Now she enjoys volunteering as a reading tutor. She also spends time crafting and traveling with her husband.

TABLE OF
CONTENTS

FAST FACTS

Full Name

- Barbara Pierce Bush

Birthdate

- June 8, 1925, in New York City, New York

Husband

- President George H. W. Bush

Children

- George W., John (Jeb), Marvin, Neil, and Dorothy

Years in White House

- 1989–1993

Accomplishments

- Founded the Barbara Bush **Foundation** for Family **Literacy**. This organization works to increase literacy in the United States.

- Has written four books: *C. Fred's Story*, *Barbara Bush: A Memoir*, *Millie's Book*, and *Reflections: Life after the White House*.

Chapter 1

GAINING A LIFE PARTNER

arbara and George Bush hiked through the hot sand in the desert of Saudi Arabia in 1990. Thousands of U.S. troops greeted them with cheers. Barbara's hand cramped as she signed pictures. But she couldn't think of anything else she'd rather be doing. She shook hands and gave hugs as the cameras surrounding her snapped pictures. The sun beat down on her white, curly hair as she waited in a long line to get food. She ate dinner at a table with young soldiers. As they prepared to leave, Barbara's eyes scanned the crowd. She didn't want to go. Barbara remembered a time when her husband was a soldier in World War II.

◀ George and Barbara spent Thanksgiving with U.S. troops in 1990.

Barbara and George met when she was 16 years old at a dance during Christmas vacation in 1941. She was dancing happily when a friend cut in on her dancing partner. She gave him a questioning look, wondering what he was up to. He led her toward a tall, dark-haired man and introduced her to George. When Barbara learned he wasn't a very good dancer, she agreed to just sit and talk with George away from the dance floor. She hardly noticed the songs slipping by as she and George spent time talking.

After Christmas vacation, Barbara and George went their separate ways. She went back to school. He joined the U.S. Navy. But Barbara wanted to stay in contact, so she began writing him long letters. In 1943, George became the youngest bomber pilot in the navy. He named his plane "Barbara." When George came home to visit, he and Barbara would picnic on the beach.

At Christmas in 1943, the two announced their engagement. No one in Barbara's family was surprised.

Barbara and George were married on January 6, 1945. ▶

They were married on a cold day in Rye, New York. Barbara stood in a white wedding dress at the back of a church. It was overflowing with family and friends. As her father walked her down the aisle toward George, Barbara felt her heart racing. Many years later, she said, "One of the reasons I made the most important decision of my life, to marry George Bush, is because he made me laugh. . . . That shared laughter has been one of our strongest bonds."[1]

Barbara constantly worried that George would be called back to fight in the war. When World War II was over, Barbara was thankful. Her husband would never have to fly his bomber plane again. The newlyweds did not know what was to come, but they were happy together.

◄ By 1964, the Bush family included Neil, Jeb, George W., George Sr., Dorothy, Barbara, and Marvin.

Chapter 2

FIRST LADY BARBARA BUSH

Thousands of eyes watched as Barbara took the stage at the Republican National **Convention** in 1988. Her voice rang through the microphone as she encouraged the people gathered there to support her husband for the presidency. With a twinkle in her eye, she told millions about the wonderful family man she had married. She was the first spouse ever to address the convention. That November, George was elected president.

When George took the oath of office on a cold, sunny day in 1989, Barbara looked at him with pride.

◄ Barbara listened as George took the oath of office on January 20, 1989.

After the ceremony, George and Barbara smiled and waved to thousands of **spectators** as they led the parade to the White House. Barbara later wrote, "To this day, my impressions are very vivid: lots of friends, beautiful singing, miles of people. It was thrilling."[2]

Soon after she became the First Lady, Barbara remembered a time in 1978 when she had been jogging in Houston, Texas. As the hot sun sank into her skin, Barbara felt a knot of worry in her stomach. With every step she took, she grew more concerned about the homelessness, hunger, and crime that troubled the United States.

"You can no longer say, 'The drug problem worries me' or 'Crime worries me' or 'Illiteracy worries me.' If it worries you, then you've got to do something about it. Walk out your door and help someone."[3]

—Barbara Bush

▲ Barbara traveled across the country to read to children.

Barbara had an idea to help the country. All those things "would be better if more people could read, write, and **comprehend**."[4] As the First Lady, Barbara chose to work on improving literacy in the United States.

In 1989, Barbara started the Barbara Bush Foundation for Family Literacy. The organization created programs to teach people how to read. The foundation set up centers all over the country. Teachers, civic leaders, and volunteers taught reading and writing. Children and their parents often learned together. Barbara appeared on television many times to promote her cause. She talked about how important it was to learn to read.

Barbara thought that being First Lady was the best job in America. But her role came to an end in 1992 after George lost the presidential election. The family packed up their things and prepared to leave the White House. Before leaving, Barbara walked down hallways and past rooms that had been her home for the last four years. She recalled countless memories she had made there. With tears in her eyes, Barbara hugged the staff and said goodbye. Then she started looking toward the next chapter of her life.

Barbara welcomed the new First Lady, Hillary Clinton, into the ▶
White House after George lost the presidential election.

Chapter 3

LEAVING A LEGACY

Tears welled up in Barbara's eyes as she passed a pick-up truck on the highway. Two people stood in the back with a sign. It said, "Welcome home George and Barbara."[5] The Bush family had just left Washington, DC, for their new home in Maine. It was a wonderful welcome to their new neighborhood.

Barbara was thankful for the time she could now spend with her large family. But she still wanted to give back to the country. Feeling energized, she accepted the position of **honorary** chair of the Barbara Bush Foundation for Family Literacy. Every year, she hosted its annual fund-raiser, "A Celebration of Reading." She invited famous authors to read from their latest books.

◄ Barbara visited bookstores to encourage children to read.

▲ George W. Bush (right) became president in 2001.

Money raised at the event helped fund programs run by the foundation.

Although she was proud of her work, she believed her children would be her **legacy**. They did not disappoint her. In 1999, her son Jeb was sworn in as governor of Florida. Her daughter Dorothy became cochair of the Barbara Bush Foundation for Family Literacy. And in 2000, with pride in her eyes, Barbara watched as her son George W. was elected president. Until then only one other woman, Abigail Adams, had been both the wife and the mother of presidents.

Barbara made history that day. Her time in and out of the White House proved she would leave behind a lasting effect on the country.

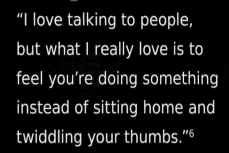

"I love talking to people, but what I really love is to feel you're doing something instead of sitting home and twiddling your thumbs."[6]

—*Barbara Bush*

THINK ABOUT IT

- What are some problems the United States faces today? If you were the president's spouse, what would your cause be?
- What are some ways that reading has had an impact on your own life?
- Barbara wanted to help people learn to read. Do you think it's the responsibility of the president and First Lady to help everyone despite their education level or income?

GLOSSARY

comprehend (kom-pri-HEND): To comprehend means to understand something. Barbara wants children to comprehend literature.

convention (con-VEN-shun): A convention is a large meeting, especially for members of a political party looking to select someone for a political office. Barbara spoke at the Republican National Convention.

foundation (foun-DAY-shun): A foundation is an organization set up to help a cause. Barbara's foundation helped people learn to read and write.

honorary (ON-uh-rayr-ee): Honorary means to be given as an honor for outstanding service. Barbara is the honorary chair of her literacy foundation.

legacy (LEG-uh-see): A legacy is something important that is passed down or remembered from one generation to the next. Barbara hopes her legacy will be her children.

literacy (LIT-ur-uh-see): Literacy is the ability to read and write. Barbara promoted literacy throughout the country.

spectators (SPEK-tay-turs): Spectators are people who look on or watch. Barbara waved to spectators during a parade.

SOURCE NOTES

1. "'No One Can Say What Your True Colors Will Be . . .'" *Los Angeles Times*. Los Angeles Times, 2 June 1990. Web. 22 June 2017.

2. Barbara Bush. *Barbara Bush: A Memoir*. New York, NY: Scribner, 1994. Print. 260.

3. "Barbara Bush." *Presidential-Power*. Siteseen Ltd., n.d. Web. 22 June 2017.

4. Barbara Bush. *Barbara Bush: A Memoir*. New York, NY: Scribner, 1994. Print. 145.

5. Ibid. 4.

6. Judy Keen. "Bush Matriarch Agonizes through Campaign." *USA Today*. USA Today. 31 Aug. 2004. Web. 22 June 2017.

TO LEARN MORE

Books

Haskell, L. S. *George W. Bush*. Mankato, MN: The Child's World, 2017.

Krull, Kathleen. *A Kids' Guide to America's First Ladies*. New York, NY: HarperCollins, 2017.

Pastan, Amy. *First Ladies*. New York, NY: DK Publishing, 2017.

Web Sites

Visit our Web site for links about Barbara Bush:

childsworld.com/links

Note to Parents, Teachers, and Librarians: We routinely verify our Web links to make sure they are safe and active sites. So encourage your readers to check them out!

INDEX